For my great nieces: Emilia, Ella, I
For my Grandson, Wesley
Love, Aunt Deedee/Gigi

Always let your light shine wherever
you go so others will see Jesus in you.

In the same way, let your light shine before others,
that they may see your good works and glorify your
Father in heaven.
Matthew 5:16 NKJV

Written after I played "hide-and-seek fireflies" with my great
nieces, Emilia and Ella but truly inspired by the Holy Spirit.

Spring is approaching

and all fireflies families are waking up.

They are eager to begin spreading their wings, stretching their legs, opening their hearts and sharing the light deep within them.

A new day has dawned

and now it's time for the little fireflies to awaken to this new life that is ahead of them. They have a big job to learn.

They are learning new skills.

Each firefly has a gift. Each has a *purpose.*
The babies have not yet *discovered* how to open
this gift. But they soon will.

They stick close to home for now because they know that once summer arrives they will be very busy. The nights are full of *wonder*.

Time passes and the tiny fireflies grow
stronger each day. Their wings gain strength.

They can fly for longer periods of time and
yet they still can't glow.

Phoebe is one of those that works hard to be the best firefly. She doesn't know what it means yet but she wants to do her very best.

Then it happens! Summer arrives.
They *witness* a beautiful summer evening.
A warm, gentle breeze blows.

The baby fireflies see their parents
flying all around.

The little ones notice a beautiful glow.
This is what the gift is! The glow! Where there was darkness,
now there is light!
It's *spectacular*.
Phoebe feels *breathless*.
She wants to be just like the big fireflies.
But how?

People are chasing after the light.
There is *excitement* all around.
Everyone *desires* the light.
They're drawn to the light.
They can't help themselves.

Phoebe is *impatient* and flies out trying to glow.

She comes back home *frustrated, embarrassed,* and *exhausted.*

When her parents return from an exciting evening, Phoebe explains just how she tried to glow.

Her parents describe how glowing has to be
something for others and not for herself.
It's to draw others to the light. Not because of
her but because of the light. She will only glow
when she's doing it for someone else.

Night after night Phoebe tries to glow.
But every night she cannot glow.

After one night of many attempts,
Phoebe sits on a bush *discouraged*.

A young boy who is lost in the park sits near the same bush crying because he cannot find his way back to his family.

Phoebe hears the young boy crying.

Out of love for the boy,
she flies in and around his body.

All of a sudden she begins to glow.
Her heart has changed!

The boy sees her and sits up!
His tears stop. For a moment he forgets what
is happening. All he can do is look at Phoebe.
He becomes *captivated* by the light.
She starts to fly and he follows.

She can hear people calling for him.
Phoebe leads the boy right to his family.
Her light guided his way.

Now Phoebe understands!
It wasn't about her after all.

It's always been about the light and
leading others by the light.

Phoebe makes it back home to share her days adventure with her family. She is overjoyed with her new found understanding of just how important being a firefly is!

From that day on, Phoebe knows she needs to shine as bright as she can for others so they too can see the light deep within her. And just maybe, someone else may need to be led home.